FOUL LINE

1st base coach

dugout

backstop

grass line

6 ft.

90 ft.

1st baseman

2nd baseman

INFIELD

60 ft. 6 in.

pitcher

umpire

95 ft.

catcher

batter

shortstop

3rd baseman

90 ft.

grass line

3rd base coach

dugout

FOUL LINE

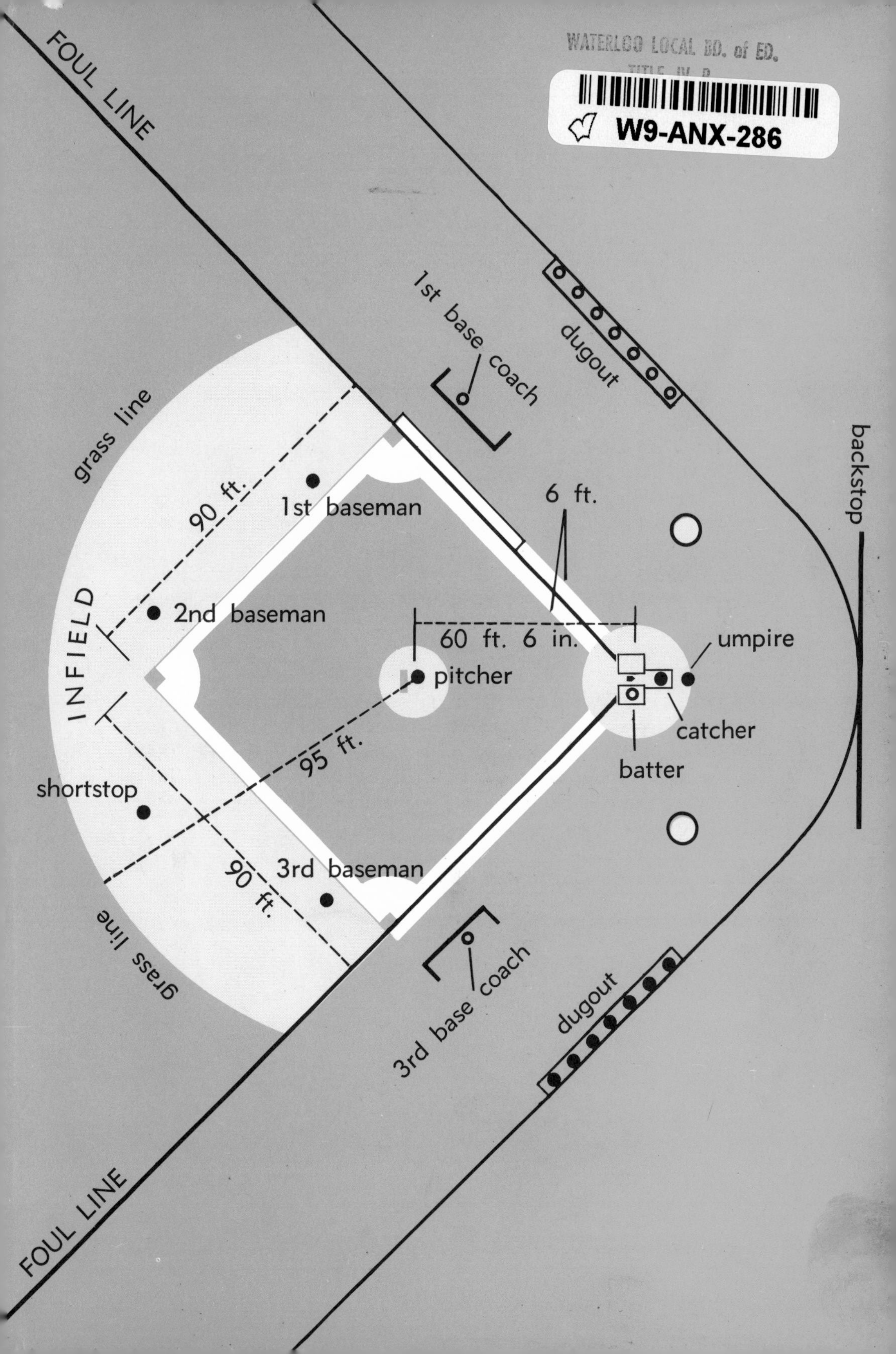

PEOPLE WHO HELPED WITH THIS BOOK

Many people helped in the writing of this book. I am especially grateful for advice from Bob Feller, Carl Hubbell, Mrs. Howard J. Ehmke, Lester D. Ehmke and from my personal third base coach: Dort Darrah Reeder.

The following former major league baseball players gave me information: Cy Slapnicka, Frank Frisch, Hans Lobert, Bing Miller, Eric Tipton, Jim Hegan and Ethan Allen.

Expert sportswriters interested themselves and pitched in: Ed Pollock, Red Smith, Dan Daniel, John Kieran, Tom Meany, Tim Cohane, John Drebinger, Hal Rosenthal and Larry Robinson.

I also thank: Eddie Brannick, of the San Francisco Giants; Tom Campion, Sr., of Bronxville, New York; Stan Lomax, radio broadcaster of WOR, New York; Leonard Orth, of Cedar Rapids, Iowa; Bob Fishel, of the New York Yankees; Betty Braxton and Marilyn Evers, of Scarsdale, New York; Nancy Harlow and Charlotte Snyder, of the U.S.M.A. Library, West Point, New York.

I am grateful, too, for help from the New York *Times* and the Philadelphia *Bulletin*.

RED REEDER

West Point
New York

THREE GREAT PITCHERS

ON THE MOUND

BY COLONEL RED REEDER

ILLUSTRATED BY AL FIORENTINO

920

GARRARD PUBLISHING COMPANY
CHAMPAIGN, ILLINOIS

For
JOHN B. (HANS) LOBERT
Instructor and friend
Major league player, manager, coach, scout
and
Baseball coach of the West Point cadets: 1918–1925

Photo credits:

N. Y. Daily News Photo: pp. 29, 36, 63, 86
Sy Seidman: pp. 4, 87
United Press International Photo: pp. 4, 20, 27, 30, 44, 50, 51, 77, 87, 94
Wide World Photos: pp. 4, 8, 23, 32, 34, 35, 38, 52, 64, 65, 66

Contents

Bob Feller

Howard Ehmke

Carl Hubbell

About Pitching . . .

This is the story of three expert pitchers:

> Bob Feller
>
> Carl Hubbell
>
> Howard Ehmke

A friend said to me, "Rapid Robert Feller, the fireball artist—I know him. And King Carl Hubbell—Carl had a famous screwball. They called him the 'Meal Ticket.' But why are you telling the story of Howard Ehmke?"

"Do you know what happened in the first game of the 1929 World Series?" I asked.

"No," said my friend.

"Well," I said, "that's why I am writing about Ehmke."

Pitching is one of the most difficult forms of athletics. Everyone who runs a team worries about pitching. Because it is vital to baseball, I wrote to the expert sportswriter, Dan Daniel, of the New York *World-Telegram*, and asked, "How important is pitching?"

"If anyone should know," Daniel answered, "it would be Connie Mack. I'd rely on his judgment. He managed Philadelphia for fifty years. Once I heard him talk about this with Babe Ruth and some writers.

"Ruth had banged out a homer that day. Connie Mack said, 'Pitching is 65% of the game.' Babe Ruth threw back his head and laughed. 'It's not that important,' he said. 'I know. I once was a pitcher.' Some of us sportswriters laughed, too. But the more we thought about it the more we respected Connie Mack's opinion. Today pitching is recognized as 85% of the game."

When pitchers Bob Feller, Carl Hubbell and Howard Ehmke were at their best, their value to their teams was even greater.

Bob Feller, Fireballer

A seventeen-year-old boy was warming up for the Cleveland Indians. His fast ball sped to the catcher's mitt and made it *pop*!

The Indians were playing an exhibition game in July 1936, against the St. Louis Cardinals. Everyone had heard stories about the young fireballer, Bob Feller. But few had seen him play.

Frank Frisch, star infielder and manager of the Cardinals, kept his eye on Feller.

Feller wound up, tossed his left leg waist high, and sent a fast ball zinging toward the plate. Catcher Steve O'Neill caught the ball squarely in the center of his mitt. The smack of the ball sounded like a giant firecracker.

Manager Frisch tugged at the red visor of his Cardinal cap. "This Bob Feller is the fastest pitcher I ever saw," he said.

"What about Walter Johnson, the Big Train, who pitched for Washington?" a reporter asked.

"Saw 'em both," Frisch said. "Hard to answer. Johnson just kept firing his fast ball at you. Feller's dangerously fast. And if he works up a curve, good night! If I had to bat against this boy my average would drop a few points."

Feller and Johnson were two of the fastest pitchers who ever lived. Once, before a game in Cleveland, a U. S. Army measuring device timed Bob Feller's fast ball at 98.6 miles per hour, or, one-third of a second from the mound to home plate.

Before that day against the Cardinals, few people had heard of Bob Feller. After he struck out eight Cardinals in three innings, fans and ballplayers everywhere began to talk about him.

A few weeks after that, the Cleveland manager, Steve O'Neill, said to Feller, "I'm starting you today, Bob. You can beat the Browns without hurting yourself."

Bob knew that the St. Louis Browns were in seventh place in the American League. He also knew that there would be about 10,000 people at the game. He felt nervous, starting his first major league game. Suppose some of those Browns got on base and started stealing?

When the game began Bob's nervousness left him. The Browns could not hit his pitches. He started striking them out. He had never felt better. He wished that his father were there. When the game ended, Manager O'Neill and the players pounded his back. Bob had struck out fifteen St. Louis Browns.

Three weeks later the husky youngster struck out seventeen players on the Philadelphia Athletics with his fireball. Bob Feller was mowing down major-leaguers at an unheard of rate, and he had not even played minor league ball.

Feller was born on a farm near Van Meter, Iowa in 1918.

When he was big enough, he helped his father on the farm. One of Bob's duties was to carry pails of water from the Raccoon River for the cows. This hard work gave Bob powerful arms.

With his dad, he labored in the fields. They looked forward to the evenings, when they could play catch. Mr. Feller loved baseball. He wanted to see Bob become a fine player—a big-leaguer.

Mrs. Feller was a good cook, and when work was done she called her family to supper. "But, Mother," Bob would say, "we want to play ball."

"I'll fix this," Mr. Feller said. He rigged two lights near the barn. Under them, after supper, he threw grounders for Bob to field. He also taught Bob how to bat.

One day Mr. Feller watched Bob throwing a rubber ball against the house

and catching the rebound. Bob had a strong, easy throwing motion.

"I think you have the power to make the big leagues."

Mr. Feller said, "You know, Bob, I think you'll go farther in baseball if you become a pitcher. What do you think?"

"It's all right with me, Dad."

Bob believed wholeheartedly in his father.

So together they worked on pitching.

Mr. Feller bought a book on how to play baseball and they studied it. He taught Bob how to take the two positions on the pitcher's rubber. He taught him how to wind up. But the most important thing he taught him was about himself.

"I want to tell you something about pitching," Mr. Feller said one evening. "A pitcher has to have control. I mean not only control of the ball, but of himself. A real champion is modest. There will be times when you're pitching and a team-mate's error will lose the game. Or a batter will hit your best pitch. You play ball to win, but I want you to be great even in defeat. I want you always to be a true sportsman."

Mr. Feller built a diamond on his farm. Bob helped. His dad laid out the bases and they put up a scoreboard. Then Mr. Feller talked to boys who liked to play baseball.

He drove them in his car to the farm where the boys played together, and Mr. Feller practiced with them. When they became a real team, he invited other teams to come to the farm and play. Admission was 35 cents.

In addition, Bob played on another team, in the town of Adel. Soon word got around that the boy was a good pitcher.

When Bob was fourteen, Mr. Feller thought he should have a chance to play faster baseball. "I'm driving to Des Moines to talk to those American Legion men," Mr. Feller said. When he returned he reported happily, "I got a chance for you to try out."

Bob was happy, too. He soon became the best pitcher in the American Legion league. Sometimes he wondered if a big league scout would ever come to see him play, and he kept on pitching. Then his father got

Bob a chance to play on the Farmer's Union Insurance team. These games went nine innings instead of seven. It was more exciting baseball and rougher on pitchers.

One day a man came to the Feller farm. "Slapnicka is my name," he said to Mr. Feller. "I'm with the Cleveland Indians. I'd like to see your son pitch. I hear he likes baseball."

Mr. Feller turned to Bob. Bob was so excited he could hardly answer. He *loved* baseball.

"So you want to see Bob pitch?" Mr. Feller asked. "Well, he's got a fast ball that zooms upward as it nears the batter."

"That's just what a fast pitch should do," Mr. Slapnicka said. "When will he pitch?"

"Sunday in Des Moines," Mr. Feller said. "Bob's striking out an average of nineteen men a game."

On Sunday, Bob pitched splendidly. Mr.

Slapnicka watched him from left field and from back of the plate.

On the way home, Mr. Feller was silent. Finally he said, "Bob, I do not want to push you into being a pro ballplayer. I'll always help you as hard as I'm able, but this must be your decision. I want you to decide what you want to be."

Bob slipped his arm about his dad. It was hard to talk. "I want to be a big league pitcher. And I'm sure I can be one."

Later that evening Mr. Slapnicka came to the farm. The two men agreed that Bob should play minor league baseball first.

"A young fellow needs experience," Mr. Slapnicka explained. "The minors—that's the place to get it. Not before big crowds."

Mr. Slapnicka brought out an important looking paper from his pocket. "This is a contract," he said. "Trust me."

"I trust you," Mr. Feller said.

"I do, too," Bob added.

Bob signs major league contract as his proud father (right) and Slapnicka (left) look on.

"Let Bob sign this. Then in the spring he'll pitch in North Dakota."

Bob felt wonderful. His brown eyes sparkled. Now he could picture himself in the Cleveland Indian uniform.

"What about school?" Bob's mother asked. "He's a fine student—president of the junior class in high school. I want him to graduate."

"We do, too," the scout said.

"I can study in the off season," Bob said.

Bob studied long hours that winter and he looked forward to spring. But a sore arm ended Bob's minor league career before it began. He never reported to the North Dakota team.

Although Mr. Slapnicka was worried about Bob's arm, he was sure Bob was going to be a great pitcher. He took Bob to Cleveland. Even if Bob couldn't pitch right away, Mr. Slapnicka wanted to keep an eye on him. This caused trouble. The North Dakota people claimed a "foul." *They* wanted Bob. But Bob began to pitch for Cleveland.

It was the summer of 1936—the same summer he struck out eight St. Louis Cardinals in three innings. That season he won five games and lost three.

In December, Judge Landis, the Baseball Commissioner, sent for Bob and his dad. The judge ruled that the Dakota claim was correct. He ordered the Cleveland club to pay the North Dakota team $7,500.

The whole Feller family was glad the argument was finally settled. Mr. Feller and Bob were happy because Bob would play big league ball again. Mrs. Feller was pleased because Bob had returned to high school in the fall. Also, she was happy because he would be tutored when he went back to pitch for Cleveland.

Bob worked hard to develop a great curve ball as a pitcher for the Cleveland Indians.

Bob began to learn more about baseball. Mr. Slapnicka and the Cleveland pitching coach, Mel Harder, helped. They spent long hours in the spring coaching him. They worked in the Cleveland stadium when no one else was there.

"Let me see your fast one, then a curve," Mr. Slapnicka said.

Bob fired a scorcher at the catcher, then threw his curve.

"Fastest pitch I ever saw," Mr. Slapnicka said. "But that curve! Has to be sharper. A better curve will keep the batters off balance. Well-rounded pitchers need more than one great pitch."

"How can I make it break more?" Bob asked.

"Loosen your wrist. Give the ball more spin with your fingers," Mr. Slapnicka said.

Bob tried, and the ball broke downward as it neared the catcher.

"Fine!" Mr. Slapnicka said.

Two great catchers also coached Bob, Wally Schang and John Bassler. Bob's curve began to break sharply. After three months he could make the ball break exactly where he wanted.

Bob asked many questions of the four experienced men helping him. "When I get out in front of a crowd," Bob said, "I feel tight. My heart beats faster. Why is that?"

"Nothing unusual," Slapnicka said. "Every new player feels that way. You have to gain confidence."

"How do I do that?"

"I'm telling you that you're as good as any pitcher in the game—better than most," Mr. Slapnicka said. "You can believe that."

Bob's face broke into his modest grin. He appreciated Mr. Slapnicka's interest.

"You're going to be one of the best pitchers that ever wore a toeplate," Mr. Slapnicka said. "Calm down. But always remember you have *three* weapons against the batters—an amazing fast ball, a wonderful curve and control. The more you work, the more you believe in yourself, the better you'll be."

Bob added a *fourth* weapon—a change of pace. He had grown up as a pitcher. Batters feared him.

Near the end of the 1937 season, Bob was facing Joe Cronin, an ace hitter for the Boston Red Sox. Cronin swung at two of Bob's pitches and missed. Bob sent his fast ball over the plate. Cronin kept his bat on his shoulder.

"Strike three!" the umpire said.

"I didn't see it," Cronin said to the umpire. "Did you?"

Manager Vitt demonstrates correct pitching stance to Feller. New rule allowed pitcher to stand with one foot back of the rubber.

The American League record for the most strikeouts in a game was seventeen. Bob was trying to break it. He fanned sixteen Red Sox that day, almost tying the record. The next year Bob broke it by fanning eighteen Detroit Tigers.

In 1939, he was the best pitcher in the league. He won 24 and lost 9. He was selected to play in the All-Star game.

On the first day of the 1940 season, Manager Oscar Vitt readied his Indians for the opening game against Chicago. A raw wind lashed the whitecaps on Lake Michigan. The White Sox looked snappy in their infield drill.

"All right, Bob," Manager Vitt said. "Warm up!"

Bob was delighted. His family was watching from the stands.

Catcher Hemsley said, "Just throw fast ones, Bob. Okay?"

In the ninth, every fan was sitting on the edge of his seat. Bob had not yet allowed one hit. The Indians were not talking to him. They were afraid that if they talked they would jinx him. The score stood 1-0 in favor of Cleveland.

Up to the plate walked Luke Appling, star Chicago shortstop. He had batted .314 the year before. Most of the White Sox

fans were rooting for Bob to strike the batter out. Luke sliced ten fouls. Finally Bob walked him. The crowd groaned.

Taffy Wright, a left-handed .300 hitter, stepped into the batter's box. Some fans screamed for Taffy to get a hit and tie the score. The catcher signaled. Bob threw his fast ball. Taffy banged a hard grounder.

The Indian second baseman scooped it up and flipped to first to retire the side. Bob leaped for joy. He had pitched the first no-hit opening game in the history of the American League.

After their unusual start, many expected the Indians to win the pennant. But trouble set in.

The Cleveland Indians celebrate Feller's no-hit game on opening day in 1940.

It centered on Manager Vitt. He was a high-strung man. He had played on the Detroit Tigers for ten years with Ty Cobb. Vitt had some of Cobb's characteristics. Both were fierce competitors.

The Indians felt that Vitt disliked the way they played. He was often abrupt with them. For example, once when pitcher Mel Harder was knocked out of the box, Vitt was sarcastic. On the mound, Vitt said, "Harder, when are you going to earn your salary?"

This hurt Harder. He felt he had given his best.

The Indians talked the situation over. A committee of players went to the president of the club. They felt the team could play better under a new manager. Bob was on the committee, but he was not their spokesman.

The sportswriters heard about the

players' feelings toward Vitt. The newspapers talked of the "Vitt Rebellion" and called the players the "Cry Babies."

The name stuck. Everywhere, the fans shouted, "Cry Babies!" In some parks they placed babies' milk bottles and diapers on the Cleveland dugout. The players felt the fans were unjust, but they concentrated on playing baseball.

When the season neared its end, the race for the American League championship narrowed to the Detroit Tigers and the Indians. Cleveland fans turned out in large numbers to cheer their team. Bob won game after game. He seemed invincible. But after his twenty-seventh win of the season he was tired.

In late September, the Indians played a key game with the Tigers. Thousands came to see it. Vitt chose Bob to pitch. The Indians had to win or finish in second place. Bob pitched his hardest. He allowed only three hits, but lost 2-0. As he took off his uniform, he felt awful. It was a bitter day, but he did not complain. He was the sportsman his father wanted him to be.

The following year, under a new manager, Bob again was the top pitcher in the league. His season record was 25 wins and 13 losses.

But, two months after the season ended, life changed for almost every American. The Japanese dropped bombs on Pearl Harbor. The date was December 7, 1941.

Two days later, Bob kissed his family good-by. He enlisted in the United States Navy. The Navy recognized his ability and trained him in gunnery. He was promoted to chief petty officer and sent aboard the battleship *Alabama*. The captain placed

Bob in command of an antiaircraft crew.

The sailors idolized him, but Bob kept his head. This made him even more popular.

It was a hard life. Part of the time, the battleship sailed the North Sea. It went almost to Russia. The ship and her crew also saw action in the South Pacific and the Philippines. Bob missed his family and friends very much.

Bob Feller is at bat. The scene is a jungle base somewhere in the South Pacific, 1944.

When the war was over, Bob again
pulled on his Cleveland uniform. It did not
take him long to regain his best form.
After a four year layoff, this surprised
people. In 1946, he pitched a no-hit game
against the powerful New York Yankees.
That season he struck out 348 men. It was
a new record.

Some said, "If Feller had not gone into military service, there's no telling how many records he'd have broken." But Bob would have none of that talk. He said, "I felt it was my duty to serve my country."

Bob Feller hung up his uniform for the last time in 1956. He had become the holder of many records. Twelve times he almost pitched additional no-hit games— one hit making the difference. He won 266 games for Cleveland. He lost 164. He struck out 2,588 players. In 1962, a Bob Feller plaque was placed in the Baseball Hall of Fame.

Today Bob is in the insurance business in Cleveland. The people in Adel, Iowa, in 1964, honored Bob with a plaque. They put it on a boulder in a park, close to the diamond where he played as a boy. The bronze plaque shows the arm of a pitcher. This is for Bob Feller, true sportsman.

Carl Hubbell,
Control Pitcher

"Operator, I want to speak to Manager John J. McGraw of the Giant baseball team. He's in New York City." The caller was Giant scout Dick Kinsella. He waited nervously in the heat of the Texas summer for the call to go through.

Long distance telephoning was still a novelty in 1928. When McGraw answered, Kinsella felt he had to shout to be heard in New York. "Mac, this is Dick Kinsella calling from Houston. I think I saw a great pitcher today. He pitches now for Beaumont in the Texas League. Pitched eleven smart innings. Beat Houston, one to zero."

"What's his name?"

"Carl Hubbell. Twenty-five years old. Slightly over six feet. Strong and wiry. Wonderful control. Cool as a watermelon."

"Right or left?" McGraw asked.

"Left-hander. Tried out with Detroit but they sent him back to the minors. Sometimes throws a screwball. The Detroit coaches told him it would ruin his arm."

McGraw said, "Can this Hubbell help us?"

Kinsella chuckled at his friend McGraw. "I wouldn't call from Texas just to chat about the weather."

"Put him on the express to Chicago. I'll meet him at the Auditorium Hotel."

"He'll be on the night train."

40

In Chicago, Carl Hubbell felt nervous as he took an elevator to McGraw's suite. He also felt a strong desire to be a big-leaguer. *If I cannot make the major leagues*, he had vowed to himself, *I'll quit baseball. I won't pitch in the minors.*

Carl wondered about Manager McGraw. There were stories about his harshness.

But the manager put him at ease. He shook hands warmly. "Have a seat, Carl.

Glad to have you with the New York Giants. Tell me about yourself."

Carl's black eyebrows knitted, making him look a bit like Abraham Lincoln. "I'm from a farm near Meeker, Oklahoma," he drawled. "Had a hard time getting started as a pitcher. Didn't have a chance to play ball till my last two years of high school."

"How'd that happen?"

Carl grinned. "Sir, there weren't enough boys in our high school for a team until that time."

"I know you throw a screwball," the manager said. "The greatest pitcher the Giants ever had, Christy Mathewson, threw a fadeaway. Absolutely puzzled the hitters. It broke away from left-handed batters because he threw right-handed. Your screwball is just the opposite. It curves away from right-hand hitters. Correct?"

"Yes, sir," Carl replied.

"Well, it's strictly up to you whether or not you throw it." From the way the manager said this, Carl knew what he meant. McGraw wanted results. Now it was up to Carl.

"I'm assigning you Mel Ott as a roommate. He's from Louisiana and has a drawl thicker than yours."

Both men laughed. Carl liked McGraw.

"Take a few days to rest up," McGraw said. "You'll start against the Pirates."

But the Pittsburgh batters, headed by "Big Poison" Waner and his brother, "Little Poison," and "Pie" Traynor, were too much for Carl. The Pirates knocked him out of the box in the second inning. Carl lost the game 7-5. He felt worried.

After the game, McGraw took him to one side and said, "You didn't pitch too badly. I think you're going to stay with us."

Carl's spirits rose. That night his supper

Carl Hubbell and the great slugger, Mel Ott, were roommates and then became good friends.

tasted surprisingly good. Then he thought that perhaps McGraw was spoofing him. Carl talked the matter over with Mel Ott.

"He knows how much we need good pitching to catch the Cardinals," Mel drawled. "If there is anyone in baseball who means what he says, it's Mr. McGraw."

The Giants were in second place, making a drive for the pennant. Just ahead were the St. Louis Cardinals. Every Giant was playing his hardest in every game.

Carl found relief from the intense pressure in his friendship with Mel Ott, home run hitter. Ott, quiet and modest as Carl, was short and powerful. At night when the two friends were in their beds they talked baseball. Mel encouraged Carl.

"I like your control," Mel said. "When you give a walk it's an event."

"Yes," said Carl, "but those right-hand batters are hitting me. My curve breaks in on them. The good right-handers can pull it to left field."

"Stop worrying and go to sleep. I'll bet you even pitch in your dreams."

"Only to left-handers. Pleasant dreams." Carl laughed.

A few days later the Giants were playing the Cardinals. In a meeting before the game, McGraw had warned the team about Chick Hafey, right-handed batter.

"Chick Hafey is pounding the ball. Latest

average I have on him is .337. Quick wrists. Play him to pull."

Carl was pitching against the Redbirds. The first two batters singled. Up came Hafey. Carl pitched carefully. The count was three balls and one strike. "Shanty" Hogan, Carl's catcher, signaled for a fast ball. Carl threw his screwball. Hafey swung, but the ball curved away. He missed. Hafey called, "Time!" stepped out of the box, and cleaned his glasses.

Shanty Hogan gave Carl the fast-ball sign again. Again Carl threw his screw-ball. It broke sharply away from Hafey and downward. Hafey swung. Up went the umpire's arm. "Strike three!"

In the dugout after the inning, Hogan beamed. "That was great, Carl! That funny pitch will drive these right-hand batters crazy."

McGraw walked up. He tried to conceal his delight, but his blue eyes sparkled.

"What did you throw to Hafey?" he asked.

"Screwball," Carl said.

The manager took a drink of water from the cooler, smiled and sat down. Carl Hubbell, in deciding to feature his screwball, was setting a course that would land him in the Hall of Fame.

The next season Carl pitched a no-hit, no-run game against the Pirates. He felt great, and his screwball was helping him. So was his control. He walked few batters.

The fast ball is gripped with the thumb and first two fingers, as shown below. The ball comes straight off the pitcher's fingers.

McGraw liked this. "Fine!" he said to Carl. "Make them *hit* to get on."

Carl wrote to a friend who asked him about the key to good control. "Concentration is the secret. I let nothing upset me when I am thinking about where I am going to throw the ball. A golfer hitting a ball to a green, pictures in his mind where the ball is meant to go. I do the same thing in pitching." Carl's four years with McGraw saw constant improvement in his control.

The screwball is pitched with the same motion, but the wrist is turned sharply in toward the body. The ball is flipped with the first finger, giving it a terrific spin toward the plate.

The new Giant manager, Bill Terry, watches as Carl Hubbell warms up his arm.

But in 1932 Manager McGraw resigned because of ill health. The baseball world was shocked. It had expected him to go on and on. "Memphis Bill" Terry was appointed manager. He was a hard-hitting first baseman and a splendid fielder. Fans, writers and players wondered what changes Terry would make.

Carl felt secure. By the end of his fourth season with the Giants, he had won 59 games and lost 41.

Manager Terry surprised people. Due to the makeup of his squad, he thought mostly about the value of defense. Terry had a first-rate pitching staff headed by Carl. He had a new lead-off man in "Jo-Jo" Moore, who often hit the first pitch for a single. He had only two sluggers: Mel Ott and himself. A freshman shortstop, "Blondy" Ryan, supplied spark. The new catcher, "Blackie" Mancuso, was a hustler.

"We'll stress defense," Terry announced.

Bill Terry talks to the Giant team on his first day as manager at the Polo Grounds.

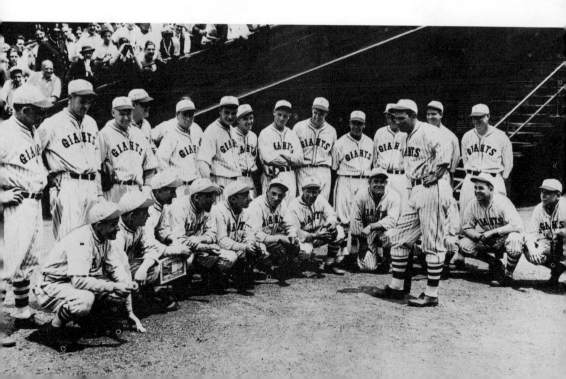

It was a good decision. Then the Giants began to roll—toward the pennant.

Before one game, Mancuso said, "Carl, you're throwing your screwball at different speeds."

"Yup," Carl replied. "I can even use it as a change of pace. I concentrate on the batters even when I'm not playing. I try to figure which speed bothers each one of them the most."

Carl Hubbell starts to wind up to pitch his famous screwball.

On a sizzling July day, Carl put on the most amazing pitching exhibition ever seen at the New York Polo Grounds. Against the Cardinals, at the end of the ninth inning, the score stood locked at 0-0.

"What do you think, Carl?" Bill Terry asked. "Do you want to stay with it?"

"Sure," Carl said. He nodded toward the Cardinals. "If 'Tex' Carleton can, I can."

But, in a few innings, Jess Haines went in to pitch for the Cardinals.

The fans sat glued to their seats. The incredible Hubbell kept right on pitching. Finally, in the bottom of the eighteenth, the Giants scored the winning run. Carl had pitched all the way. He gave up only six hits and not a single base on balls. The papers nicknamed Carl the Giants' "Meal Ticket."

Four days later, at the All-Star game, the fans stood and applauded as Carl walked to the mound. But he made only a token appearance. He was tired from his 18-inning battle.

After he'd had a rest he was back in top form. He pitched 46 1/3 innings without allowing a run.

All the Giants were inspired by Carl's great work. The shortstop, Blondy Ryan, recovering from being spiked, telegraphed Terry: AM ON MY WAY! THEY CAN'T BEAT US!

This became the team's rallying cry. The players shouted to one another, *"They can't beat us!"* And they couldn't. The Giants won the pennant.

That year Carl's record of 23 and 12 led the league. He gave up only 47 bases on balls.

In the World Series against the Senators, Carl won the first game. In the fourth game the Giants were ahead 2-1 in the last of the eleventh. But the Senators filled the bases. Bolton, a hard hitter, was up. There was only one out.

"Time!" Manager Terry called. He beckoned to Mancuso as he walked to the mound. The infielders gathered about Carl.

"We have to get out of this hole," Terry said. "I want the infield to play in on the grass, to cut a run off at the plate."

Charlie Dressen, at third base for the Giants, had an idea. "Wait!" he said. "I know this Bolton. If Carl can make him hit on the ground we can play back and get a double play."

"Can you, Carl?" Terry asked.

"I think so," Carl said.

"I'll take the chance," Terry said. "Infield, play back!"

Carl threw a screwball. Bolton smashed a hard grounder at Blondy Ryan. He fielded it to start the double play that

ended the game. The Giants took the series. It was a remarkable season. The "Meal Ticket" deserved his name. His work for the Giants meant bread and butter. Carl Hubbell seemed indestructible.

Early in the next season, however, Carl's elbow became painfully swollen. Trainers worked on his arm. X-rays showed bone chips in the elbow. "Better throw fewer screwballs," a doctor advised.

"I can stand the pain," Carl said to himself.

He pitched so well that, at mid-season, the fans chose Carl to pitch in the All-Star game.

Before the National League stars left their dressing room, Bill Terry, their manager, went over the American League batting order. The room was as quiet as a cemetery at midnight.

"Here it is," Terry said. "They have some of the best hitters in baseball: Babe Ruth, Lou Gehrig, Jimmie Foxx, Al Simmons, Joe Cronin, and Bill Dickey. You are starting, Hub. How will you pitch to Babe Ruth?"

"I'll curve my screwball in on his fists," Carl said, and left the locker room to warm up with catcher Gabby Hartnett.

Babe Ruth stood nearby. He was signing autographs for a crowd of boys. Photographers were taking the Babe's picture. He topped every player in his league in home runs. And in 1927 he had startled everyone by slamming out 60 homers in one season. Babe Ruth was a feared batter, the idol of the fans.

Now, in the first inning, Carl was to face the mighty Babe. Two American Leaguers were on base, trying to rattle Carl. He wiped his brow. The July sun seemed to have chased all the air out of the Polo Grounds.

A cheer went up from fans rooting for the American League. Babe Ruth was selecting his bat. He walked to the plate swinging three bats to loosen up his huge shoulders. Then he tossed two away. He kept a long black bat. He looked at Carl and swung the bat like a tiger lashing his tail. Chuck Klein, the Giants' right-fielder, moved back against the wall—near the bullpen.

Carl threw a screwball. It curved sharply.

Ruth swung and missed. Gabby Hartnett trotted to the mound. "Throw that thing again, Carl," he said. "The big fellow can't get around on it."

Two more screwballs broke over the plate. Ruth swung and missed, and swung and missed again. A roar went up from the National League fans. Ruth walked back to the bench with his peculiar mincing steps. The fans cheered him. He looked dramatic even striking out.

The next batter, "Columbia Lou" Gehrig, stepped into the batter's box. He dug his spikes into the clay. He was an extra-base hitter, almost as powerful as Babe Ruth. The "Iron Horse," as some called Gehrig, was batting .363. Carl struck *him* out.

American League fans begged Jimmie Foxx to get a hit. "Come on, 'Double X!'" they roared. Foxx, a line-drive hitter, also hit home runs. The year before he had banged out 48. His batting average was .334. Foxx was a hard man to fool. But Carl struck *him* out.

The National League fans stood and screamed as Carl Hubbell approached the bench. He tipped his cap modestly.

In the following inning Al Simmons, who patterned himself after Ty Cobb, walked to the plate. He was a powerful right-handed pull hitter. Carl gave him exactly the same kind of medicine.

The park seethed with excitement.

Up to the plate walked a hitter from the Washington Senators, Joe Cronin. He had batted .309 the year before. It seemed impossible that Carl could strike out another star. But Carl fanned *him*.

Bill Dickey, lanky Yankee catcher, came up. He banged out a single. Then Carl fanned pitcher Lefty Gomez to end the inning.

Millions of words have been written about Carl's strikeout of the five famous American League sluggers. But Carl prefers to think of times he helped *his* team to win.

The strain of his unusual screwball was beginning to tell. For the next two years he threw it as little as possible. But he was resourceful. He developed his curve.

Carl was still a pitcher to be feared. In 1936, he had the remarkable record of 26 and 6. In the last part of that season and in the first part of the 1937 season, he won 24 straight National League games. The *Sporting News* called him "Carl the Magnificent." Crowds came to see him pitch. The sport pages rang with praises of "King Carl."

Each year opposing batters tried to figure him out. "He doesn't overpower you," they told one another. "And he never gets excited. Almost every pitch is in the strike zone. But he'll fool you badly with that corkscrew pitch he calls a screwball." Manager Frank Frisch warned his Cardinals, "Never forget that Hubbell is great from the neck up. He can think."

In 1943, Carl ended his pitching. His record is sensational. Including World

Series play, he pitched 541 games, won 257, and lost 156. He struck out 1,709 batters. He gave only 737 bases on balls, less than two per game. Bases on balls have lost many games.

Not only was he an expert screwball pitcher, but his control also helped him and his team.

Grantland Rice, the great sportswriter, wrote, "Carl Hubbell belongs among the

Hubbell is named head of Giant farm system. Congratulating him are (from left to right): Horace Stoneham, club president; (Hubbell); Mel Ott, manager; Eddie Brannick, secretary.

Juan Marichal, first Giant pitcher since Hubbell to hurl a no-hit game, is shown with the famous southpaw. Carl is now an executive with the San Francisco club.

immortals. . . . He is the most useful left-hander in baseball history."

Other writers agreed. They elected Hubbell to the Baseball Hall of Fame in 1947.

President Horace Stoneham of the Giants placed Carl in charge of the Giants' farm system. In 1958 the team moved to the West Coast to become the San Francisco Giants. Mr. Stoneham made sure that Carl moved, too.

Howard Ehmke, Surprise Pitcher

The excitement could be felt in the air. It was like the Fourth of July. At last the Horse Shoes were getting a crack at a really first-rate baseball team—the Pittsburgh Colored Giants. The year was 1907; the place, Silver Creek, New York. Fans were coming all the way from Buffalo to see the duel. Local fans were proud of the home team's record.

Mr. and Mrs. Charles Ehmke were even prouder. They had two sons on the Silver Creek Horse Shoes. When people asked Mr. Ehmke about the game, he said, "My son Harry will hold 'em."

"What about your younger son, Howard?"

"He may be a fine pitcher some day," Mr. Ehmke said. "But, tall as he is, he's only thirteen."

The night before the game, the Ehmke family, including seven boys and four girls, sat on the porch. It was dusk. The trees in the yard looked like huge black umbrellas. Lester Ehmke said to his older brother, "Harry, they liked your pitching at Brown University, didn't they?"

Harry Ehmke nodded.

"But you know," Lester teased, "Howard may become the best pitcher in our family."

Howard felt his cheeks redden. He knew

that Harry believed that *he* was going to be the family's best pitcher.

Lester went on, "Howard practices a lot. Chucks those green apples along the creek. He can hit any target up to 90 feet. Today when we were on a lumber wagon with the horses trotting, Howard let fly an apple at a chicken about 25 yards away. Zow!"

"It didn't hurt it," Howard said.

"I'm glad of that," said Mr. Ehmke.

"Right," Lester added. "The chicken was more surprised than hurt. Howard can throw just where he aims."

"Time to turn in now, boys. Tomorrow's a big day," said Mr. Ehmke.

The next day, Pittsburgh was beating the Horse Shoes. Harry Ehmke's best pitching could not hold them. The big pitcher from Brown University was clearly worried.

About the fifth inning, a few people in the crowd began to yell for young Howard. This embarrassed him. Howard wanted to see his brother win the game.

But when another Giant cracked out a hit, the manager of the Horse Shoes turned to Howard. "Warm up! Get hot in a hurry."

Some of the crowd applauded as the tall thirteen-year-old began to loosen his arm back of the Silver Creek bench.

On his way to the pitcher's mound,
Howard was upset about Harry, but he
kept his mind on the job he had to do.

Howard threw easily and smartly. He
knew just where to pitch. His fast ball
zoomed right into the target the catcher
offered. His curve kept the Giants off
balance. But the Giants kept the lead and
won the game.

That night at the Ehmke supper table, conversation centered about the tough game. As if to excuse himself, Harry said, "I must say, Howard, that you were darn lucky." He sounded angry.

The whole family quieted.

Harry continued, "Some of those Giants hit 'you very hard."

Howard drank his milk. He could hardly swallow.

Harry barked, "Howard, college ball-players would knock you out of the park."

Howard glanced at his father. He felt his father's silent approval. "Harry," he said, "I'll be pitching for Connie Mack's Athletics some day." Then he walked out of the room.

Harry yelled after him, "You'll never see the day, pitching in the big leagues!"

From that day on, Howard Ehmke carried in his mind a picture of himself pitching for the great Philadelphia manager. He talked about his dream with his closest brother, Lester. "I'm going to wear a Philadelphia uniform," Howard liked to say. "No smoking or drinking for me."

When most of the Ehmke family moved to California, Howard became a star pitcher for Pasadena High. Then he left school and pitched for Los Angeles in the minor leagues. He was 20 years old.

Newspapers called him the "Schoolboy Phenom." Crowds came to see him. He won eight games straight. The Los Angeles team rocketed into first place. Howard had gained his full height of 6 feet 3 inches, but he wasn't strong. He looked like a tall string bean. By the time the season had ended he had won 20, lost 11, and fanned 91. Very good for a rookie—so good that the Buffalo club in the new Federal League offered him more money than Los Angeles. The rookie signed.

This was a bad mistake. The Federal League, desperately needing players, stole star athletes from the minor leagues. But people did not come to Federal League parks. Because of this, the new league died and many players had a hard time finding jobs. Howard was one of them. He felt he was being punished for playing with the Federals.

Finally Syracuse, in the International League, signed him to pitch. He won 31 games and lost 7, a league record. The manager called Howard aside. "Howard, we are selling you to the Detroit Tigers."

Howard grinned. He had made the big leagues, at last!

"When do I report?" he asked.

"Right away. The Tigers need you. They're holding down third place."

Howard felt wonderful as he pulled on his Detroit uniform. He liked Manager Jennings' freckle-faced grin. He also liked being on the Tigers' pitching staff so much that he could hardly believe what he heard next. The player at a nearby locker jeered at him. He sounded angry, just like brother Harry.

"We must be in bad shape if we have to bring up players from the sugarplum bushes." It was Ty Cobb, the greatest player in baseball. From that moment on Howard disliked Cobb. And Cobb scorned the rookie.

Howard pitched well for Jennings and Detroit. When the United States entered World War I, Howard volunteered for the Navy. He served in the submarines.

After the war he came back to play for Detroit and Hughie Jennings. In four seasons he pitched in 146 games. He won

After serving in World War I, Howard Ehmke
returned to pitch for the Detroit Tigers.

62 and lost 59. But trouble began in 1921
when Ty Cobb was made Tiger manager.

Ty Cobb's dazzling play was the talk of
baseball. He was a man with a restless
desire to be first in everything. Cobb had
a terrible temper. His fiery manner upset
many people. One of them was Howard
Ehmke. They were exact opposites. Finally,
Howard asked Cobb to trade him to another
baseball club.

"I'll be glad to do that," Cobb snapped. "To the Boston Red Sox. They are in last place."

The next April, the Red Sox opened the season in Detroit. Howard was to pitch. He bore down his hardest on his old teammates. He was so good that even Cobb could not hit his pitches. In the eighth inning, Howard wound up and threw a sidearm pitch. It hit Cobb on the knee.

"I'm sorry!" Howard called.

Cobb danced about the batter's box. He made motions as if he were going to throw his bat at Howard. "You hit me on purpose!" Cobb thundered. "I'll get you!"

The umpire waved Cobb to first base and ordered, "Play ball!"

Howard worked hard to win that game. Afterward he stayed on the field to autograph scorecards. As he walked under

the stands toward the dressing room, he found the place almost deserted. A policeman was watching boys close a hot-dog stand. No one else seemed to be there.

Suddenly, from behind a post, Cobb leaped at Howard. "Put up your fists!" Cobb shouted. Cobb socked Howard on the mouth with a hard punch.

Then Cobb tossed Howard into the dirt.

Still too surprised to fight, Howard tried to push him off. Cobb ripped open Howard's shirt and tried to choke him. Howard gasped. He could not get up.

The patrolman ran up and pulled Cobb away. "Stop!" he shouted at Cobb. "I'll run you in."

"You'll run nobody in!" Cobb howled.

Howard dusted himself off. His face smarted. Blood trickled from his lip. He went to his dressing room very angry, but cooled off when he got under the shower. He was thinking, "I made the right move in asking to be traded—even to a last place club."

Pitching for Boston was not easy. The team had few good players. Howard disliked losing so often. But it did not bother his work. In 1923, he pitched a no-hit, no-run game against Philadelphia. In the very next game he almost pitched another no-hitter against the Yankees. His record that year was 20 won, 17 lost. This was remarkable. Few pitchers have won 20 games for a last place team.

The next year Howard's 19 wins moved the Red Sox out of last place. But in 1924 Howard pulled an arm muscle pitching in a spring snowstorm, and in 1925 nothing seemed to go right. Boston was losing again. There was no letup on the last place team. Howard was tired, and his record showed it. He won only 9 games and lost 20. The Red Sox owners thought he was a has-been and traded him off to Connie Mack.

When Howard reported to "Mr. Mack," as the players called Cornelius McGillicuddy, the older man made him feel right at home. Just sitting in Connie Mack's office was a dream come true. Howard's mind raced back to the night he told his family,

"I'll be pitching for Connie Mack some day."

Mr. Mack had his black derby on the back of his head and garters on his sleeves. His gnarled hands were folded quietly on his desk.

"Glad to have you with us, Howard. How's your arm?"

Howard flexed his long right arm.

During the last week it had hurt. The muscle he had pulled in the snowstorm still bothered him. "I think I can win some games for you."

"I'm sure of it," Mr. Mack said.

Life was wonderful with the Philadelphia Athletics. The team was in third place. An extra push could move it into first. Stars played almost every position. Max Bishop was lead-off man. Because he got so many bases on balls, he was called "Camera Eye." Outfielder Al Simmons was a great hitter. Breaking in at first base and catcher was Jimmie Foxx, "Double X," a long-ball hitter. Lefty Grove's pitching was getting better with each game. Mickey Cochrane was one of the best receivers in baseball. But the best, Howard thought, was Connie Mack. The manager was kindly, quiet and daring. He had confidence in his team.

In 1926, Howard won 15 games and lost 14. The next season his record was not as good. And the following year he slumped badly. He won 9 and lost 8, playing in only 23 games. After one game, a newspaper article about the team caught his eye. It mentioned his name: "Ehmke seems to be through."

Ehmke seems to be through! He was 35—not young for a pitcher, but he did not feel old. His uniform hung in his locker. Over the heart on the shirt was the A's traditional elephant. Once John McGraw, the famous manager, had said, "The Athletics are the white elephants of the American League." That made Connie Mack laugh. He adopted the elephant as an emblem. The players liked it. It made them think of how wrong McGraw had been. "Am I like that white elephant?" Howard asked himself.

Howard's 1929 season was worse. He pitched in only 11 games. But the team was zooming. Connie Mack could place four men on the field who would be elected to the Hall of Fame: Cochrane, Simmons, Grove and Foxx.

When the Athletics cinched the American League pennant, Philadelphia went wild. Their opponents in the World Series would be the powerful Chicago Cubs.

Mickey Cochrane   Lefty Grove   Al Simmons

Jimmy Foxx

Connie Mack

The question all over Philadelphia was: Who will pitch the first game for the A's?

The Athletics had to swing around the baseball circuit one more time. When they were leaving, Connie Mack motioned Howard into his office and shut the door. Howard felt worried.

"Well, Howard," Mr. Mack said, "the time has come for us to part."

Howard swallowed. He raised his right arm. "Connie," he said—he forgot *Mr. Mack*—"I always wanted to pitch in a World Series. I have one good game left in this arm."

Connie Mack pushed back his derby. "Umm," he said. He paced the floor slowly.

A minute ticked by. "I'm telling you a secret, Howard. You are not to go with us on this trip. Let people think whatever they may. You stay and scout the Cubs when they come to town to play the

Phillies. Don't tell this to anyone. You will be the surprise pitcher in the first game of the World Series."

It was hard for Howard to sleep nights, but he kept Connie Mack's secret. When the Cubs came to town, he sat with the crowd. He studied the Chicago batters. They were powerful. They had five .300 hitters. Rogers Hornsby was batting .380.

The day before the first game in Chicago, Connie Mack told reporters, "I never pick my pitcher until the day of the game." Manager Joe McCarthy of the Cubs said little. But privately, he told the great writer Ring Lardner, "Most of the A's pitchers don't worry us. They're fast-ball pitchers. But they have another guy named Ehmke. He throws mostly soft stuff. He's the pitcher we'll see in this series."

On opening day 51,000 people struggled to get seats. The excitement was intense.

Fifteen minutes before game time, the crowd inside the stadium applauded pitcher Root, warming up for the Cubs. A band was tooting "Take Me Out to the Ball Game." Babe Ruth walked to both dugouts and shook hands with the players.

All was tense in the Philadelphia dugout. The players didn't yet know who was going to pitch. Connie Mack picked up a new baseball and walked to Ehmke. "All right, you," he said.

Outfielder Al Simmons' mouth popped open. "Mr. Mack!" he said. "You don't mean to pitch this guy, do you?"

Connie said, "Mr. Simmons, don't you wish Mr. Ehmke to pitch today?"

The big outfielder gulped. "Mr. Mack," he said, "if you want him to pitch it is all right with me."

The Cubs peered anxiously from their dugout. They too wondered who would pitch. When Howard began to warm up, only McCarthy was not surprised.

In the pressbox, writers telegraphed the message: HOWARD EHMKE A SURPRISE STARTER WILL PITCH FOR THE ATHLETICS.

Howard began to pitch in a peculiar way. He threw the ball so that the left-field bleachers became the background. To do this, he swung his pitching arm wide. This bothered the hitters for a while. Then he brought his arm around in front of his body before he let the ball go. This made the background the light-gray shirt of his uniform. He varied the time between pitches. Nothing was certain for the Cub batters. Howard's pretzel twists fooled them. They could not hold up for his slow pitches. When they did wait, Howard sensed it and threw as hard as he could.

Everyone in the park was astounded. Howard had pitched only two complete games in the pennant race. On the mound that October day he was certainly the greatest pitcher in baseball. He gave up only one walk. He fanned player after player. He struck out the great hitters: Hornsby, Hack Wilson, and Ki-Ki Cuyler— each twice.

He went to the mound in the last of the ninth feeling confident. His team had given him a three-run lead. The Cubs had not scored. A line drive knocked him off his feet. But he recovered and threw the batter out. Then the Cubs scored. The crowd went wild. Chicago still had a chance.

Up to the plate marched two pinch hitters. The first got on base on a fielder's choice. Howard fanned the second, and the game ended. He had struck out thirteen men—a new World Series record. His joyous teammates mobbed him.

Inspired by Ehmke's great pitching in the opening
game, the Athletics go on to win the 1929 Series
from the Chicago Cubs.

In the clubhouse Mr. Mack patted him on the back. Howard had never felt happier. He gathered seven baseballs that had been used in the game. Souvenirs for his family!

A reporter shouted, "Howard, we just got a wire. All Silver Creek is having a parade in your honor."

Over the cheers, Connie Mack heard a reporter ask, "Who'll pitch tomorrow, Mr. Mack?"

"I don't know," Connie said. He did not smile, but his blue eyes danced at his joke.

The room rang with laughter.

The Athletics won the series, four games to one. The Cub batters could not seem to recover from that first drubbing. Howard pitched only a few games the next year, then retired. He became a Philadelphia businessman.

Howard's World Series strikeout record stood for 24 years. In 1953, he and his wife were driving near Philadelphia. They had the radio on. Carl Erskine was on the mound for the Dodgers against the Yankees in the World Series. Erskine struck out ten batters; then eleven, twelve, and thirteen. Howard pulled the car to the side of the road. His hand trembled slightly as he tuned the radio. He and his wife could hear the roar of the crowd.

"Ehmke's record is in danger," the announcer said.

"I hope he makes it," Howard said to his wife. "I hope he breaks my record."

Erskine wound up and pitched to the next batter. A yell went up from the crowd. "Strike three!" the announcer said.

"That does it," Howard said. "I'll send my congratulations. I *know* just how Erskine feels right now."